Coral Re

Kate Riggs

CREATIVE EDUCATION
CREATIVE PAPERBACKS

seedlings

Published by Creative Education and Creative Paperbacks
P.O. Box 227, Mankato, Minnesota 56002
Creative Education and Creative Paperbacks are
imprints of The Creative Company
www.thecreativecompany.us

Design by Ellen Huber; production by Chelsey Luther
Art direction by Rita Marshall
Printed in the United States of America

Photographs by Alamy (BIOSPHOTO, Perla Copernik,
Cultura RM, Danita Delimont, Noriyuki Otani, Martin
Strmiska), Corbis (Martin Harvey), Dreamstime (Joesayhello,
Mychadre77), Getty Images (Danita Delimont, Daniela
Dirscherl), National Geographic Creative (PAUL NICKLEN,
BRIAN J. SKERRY), Shutterstock (Tischenko Irina, Eric
Isselee, John_Walker, SM2012)

Library of Congress Cataloging-in-Publication Data
Riggs, Kate.
Coral Reefs / Kate Riggs.
p. cm. — (Seedlings)
Includes bibliographical references and index.
Summary: A kindergarten-level introduction to coral reefs,
covering their growth process, behaviors, the oceans they call
home, and such defining features as their waving tentacles.
ISBN 978-1-60818-778-2 (hardcover)
ISBN 978-1-62832-398-6 (pbk)
ISBN 978-1-56660-832-9 (eBook)
This title has been submitted for
CIP processing under LCCN 2016937118.

CCSS: RI.K.1, 2, 3, 4, 5, 6, 7;
RI.1.1, 2, 3, 4, 5, 6, 7; RF.K.1, 3; RF.1.1

First Edition HC 9 8 7 6 5 4 3 2 1
First Edition PBK 9 8 7 6 5 4 3 2 1

TABLE OF CONTENTS

Hello, coral reefs!

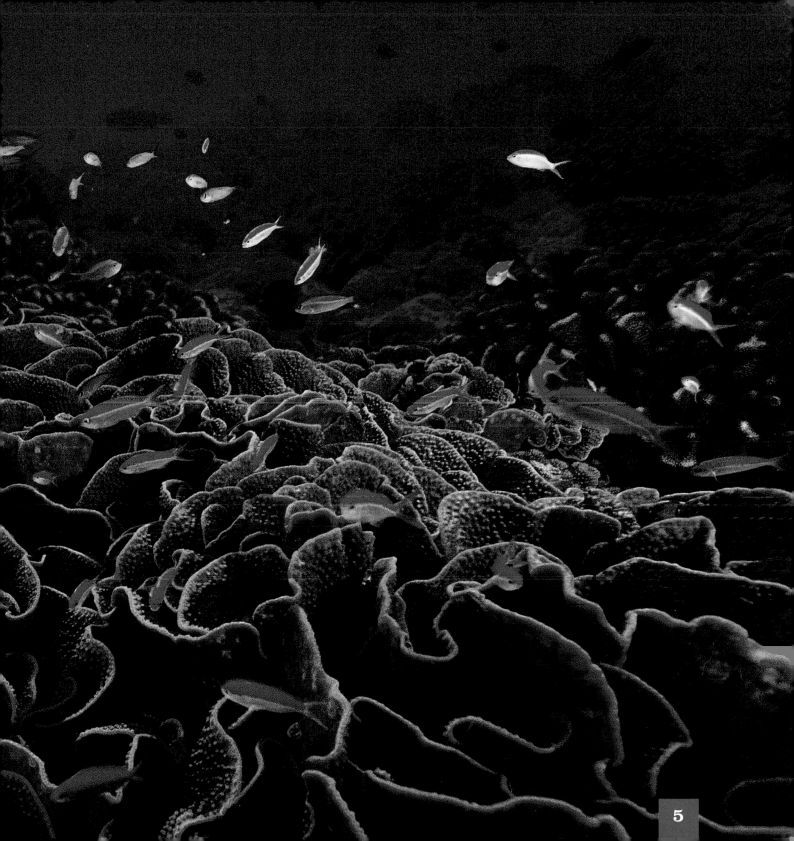

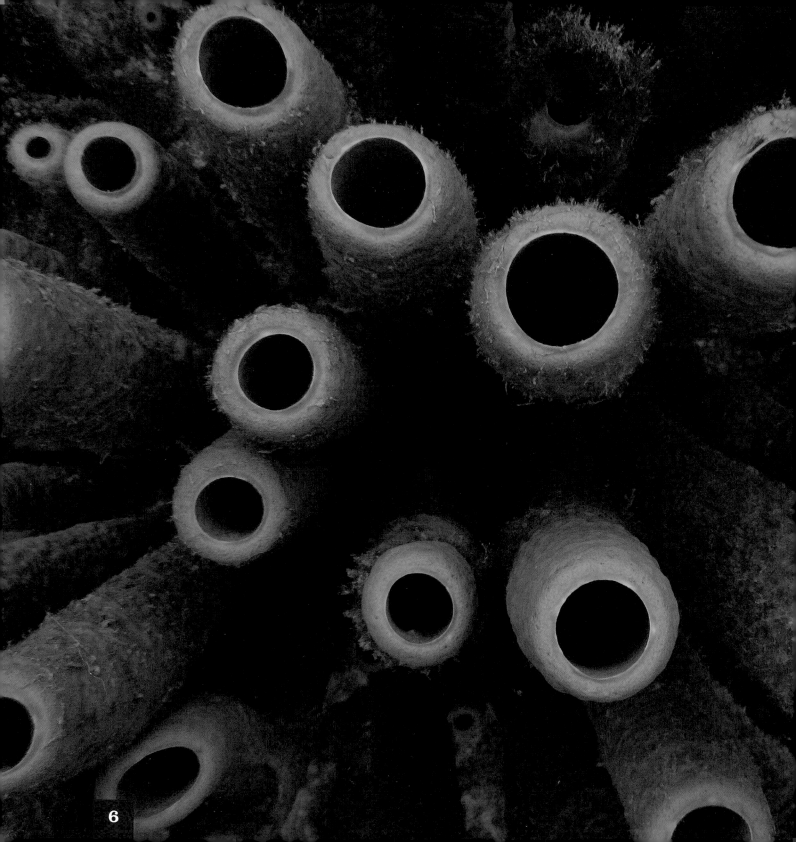

Corals are sea animals. They are shaped like tubes. They live in clear oceans.

At the top of a coral tube is the mouth. Tentacles reach up from the mouth.

They wave in the water.

There are about 1,500 kinds of coral. Many corals look like plants.

Some look like brains.

They can be
brown, green,
or other colors.

Coral tentacles catch food. Some corals eat algae. These plants may live inside corals.

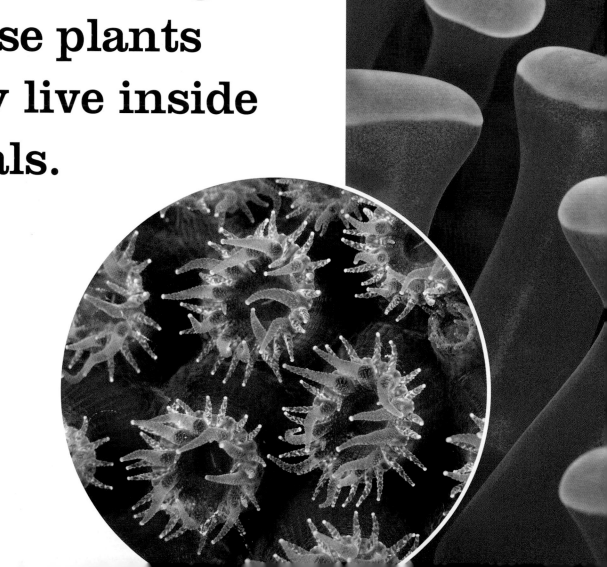

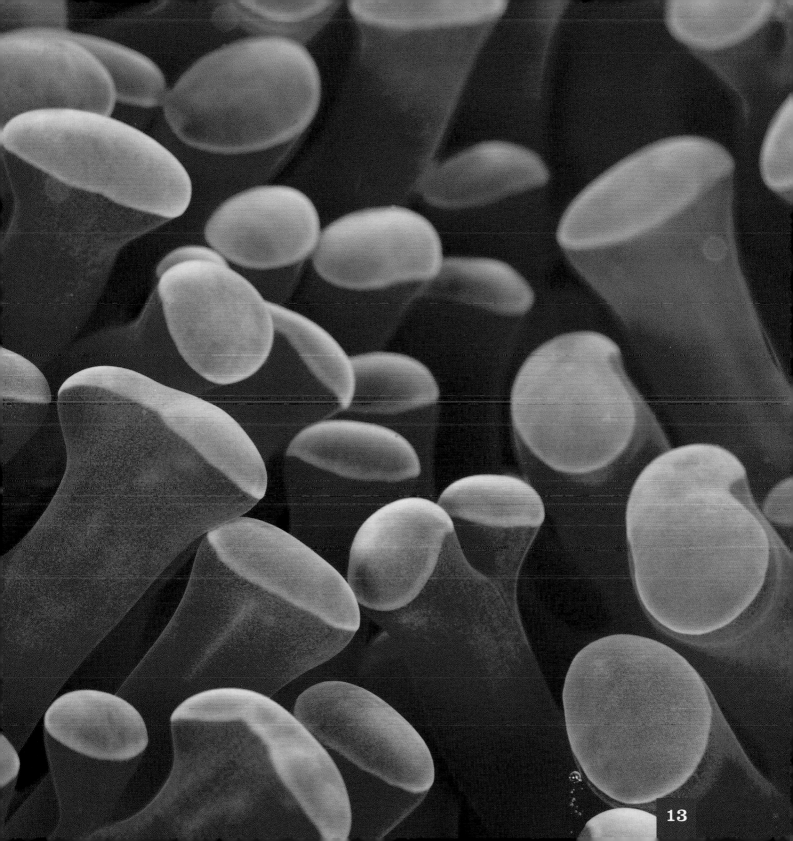

Corals live in a colony.

Coral skeletons help form a reef. Thousands of corals are there.

The Great Barrier Reef is near Australia. It is the largest coral reef in the world.

Goodbye, coral reefs!

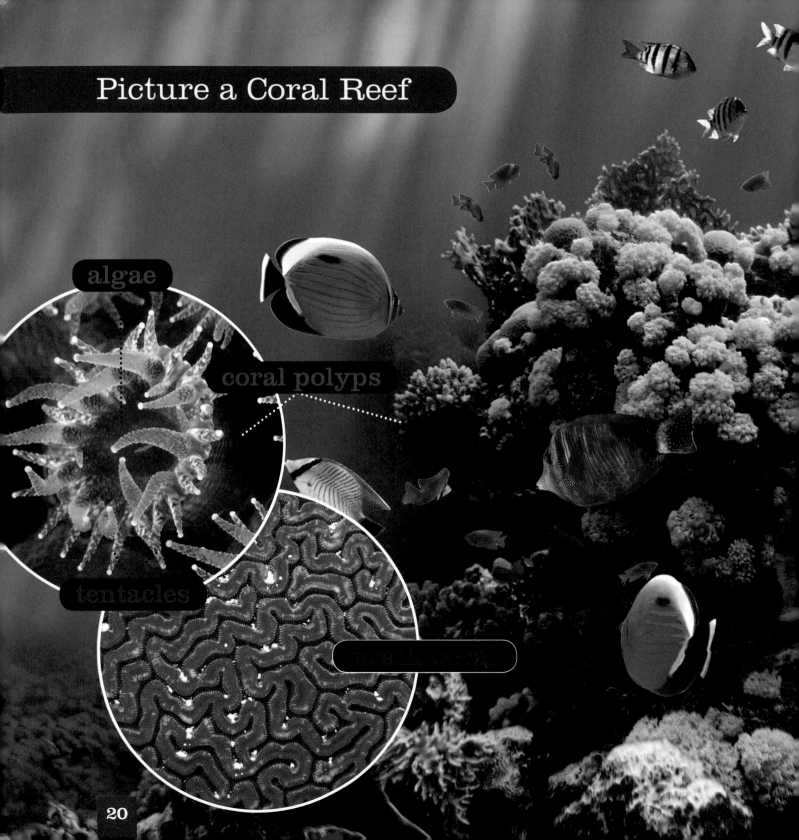

Picture a Coral Reef

algae

coral polyps

tentacles

brain coral

pufferfish

sea fan

triggerfish

parrotfish

angelfish

colony: a group of corals living together

oceans: big areas of salty water

skeletons: for corals, the rocklike bases of the corals' soft bodies

tentacles: bendable parts used for grabbing food

Read More

Heos, Bridget. *Do You Really Want to Visit a Coral Reef?*
Mankato, Minn.: Amicus, 2015.

Herriges, Ann. *Corals.*
Minneapolis: Bellwether Media, 2007.

Websites

Coral Reef Activity Book
http://www.education.noaa.gov/Special_Topics/Frequently
_Requested_Items/coral_reef_activity_book.pdf
Color pictures and do other activities related to coral reefs.

National Geographic Video: Great Barrier Reef
http://video.nationalgeographic.com/video/oceans-narrated
-by-sylvia-earle/oceans-barrier-reef
Watch a video to learn more about this special place.

Index

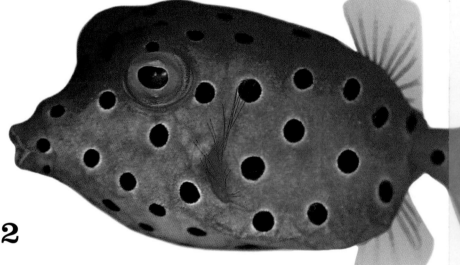